GUIDELINES FOR BIBLIOGRAPHIC DESCRIPTION OF INTERACTIVE MULTIMEDIA

The Interactive Multimedia Guidelines Review Task Force

Laurel Jizba, Chair
Eric Childress
Nancy Davey
Josephine F. Davidson
Sherry Kelley
Ann M. Sandberg-Fox
Joan Swanekamp

Committee on Cataloging: Description and Access
Cataloging and Classification Section
Association for Library Collections & Technical Services

American Library Association
Chicago and London
1994

Editor for the Task Force: Laurel Jizba

Acquisition Editor: Bonnie Smothers

Project manager: David M. Epstein

Cover design: Richmond Jones

Composition: Dianne M. Rooney

Manufacturing: Eileen Mahoney

The paper used in this publication meets the minimum requirements of American National Standard for Information Sciences—
Permanence of Paper for Printed Library Materials, ANSI Z39.
48-1984. ∞

Printed on 50-pound Scott Vellum, a pH-neutral stock, and bound
in 10-point C1S cover stock by IPC, St. Joseph, Michigan

ISBN: 0-8389-3445-5

Printed in the United States of America

98 97 96 95 94   5 4 3 2 1

PREFACE

Interactive multimedia technology represents a revolutionary step in the presentation of information in all fields of knowledge. Interactive multimedia resources are a family of rapidly evolving educational and communications tools. These tools integrate not only computer technology (including electronic textual and graphic data, and programs), but also technologies from the videorecording and sound recording industries, as well as language and concepts previously specific only to performance, creation and exhibition in film, music and other arts.

These guidelines are a response to a growing demand among catalogers for separate, practical instructions on the cataloging of interactive multimedia resources, as these resources are becoming an important part of library collections.

Objectives

These guidelines fulfill particular objectives which have been raised by many members of the cataloging community. The objectives are:

1. To facilitate and clarify the descriptive cataloging of interactive multimedia resources, addressing specific questions and areas of concern raised by the members of the American cataloging community who:

   - initially raised issues even before written guidelines were contemplated, and/or;

   - examined and experimented with early drafts of the guidelines, and/or;

   - participated in the September 1993 experimental test.

2. To balance the cataloging description by giving the cataloger the latitude necessary, given the policies of a particular cataloging agency, to highlight specific

media (audio, text, graphics, images, animation, video, etc.) similarly to the way specific chapters of AACR2R (including the *Amendments 1993* packet) highlight specific media characteristics.

3. To remain in compliance with the principles and provisions of *Anglo-American Cataloguing Rules,* second edition, 1988 revision (AACR2R), in so far as the complications of media integration in interactive multimedia resources allow compliance. Throughout these guidelines the abbreviation AACR2R is used to refer jointly to the 1988 revision of the second edition and to the packet of corrections and emendations designated *Anglo-American Cataloguing Rules, second edition, 1988 revision: Amendments 1993.*

4. To develop new cataloging instructions for the American cataloging community which address the complications of media integration in interactive multimedia resources as necessary, even though they may vary from AACR2R.

5. To provide fully cataloged examples and other appended auxiliary guidance (a request of many catalogers).

Intellectual Versus Physical Categories of Information

Interactive multimedia as defined in these guidelines represent an identifiable class of resources with shared attributes, independent of the physical carrier which delivers the information. That is, it is the characteristics of a named and integrated whole interactive multimedia work, along with information about the physical carrier or carriers, that needs primary documentation in the cataloging description. Describing entire works in this way has been termed an *intellectual* rather than a *physical* description by several experts in cataloging theory who corresponded with the Task Force. Indeed, there are chapters in AACR2R which also focus more on gathering together intellectual characteristics of an entire package of information rather than on specific physical manifestations: serials, analytics, manuscripts (particularly regarding collections), music, and cartographic materials.

Correlation with AACR2R

In addition to the two preceding discussions (the guidelines' objectives and the intellectual versus physical categories of information), catalogers may note other ways in which these guidelines differ from AACR2R:

1. The guidelines include a section titled "Additional help for identifying interactive multimedia," designed to assist catalogers by posing a number of questions and characteristic descriptive clues in case the cataloger cannot immediately identify whether or not the guidelines apply. AACR2R has no such category of instruction.

2. The guidelines include chief source instructions for the entire intellectual entity (the interactive multimedia work), which is necessary because AACR2R does not cover interactive multimedia works. While AACR2R does cover chief source information for separate physical components (see area 2 of various related chapters in Part I, AACR2R), there remains a need for instruction for the chief source of interactive multimedia works, which the guidelines provide and AACR2R does not provide.

3. Similarly, as with chief source, the guidelines explicitly provide instruction for prescribed sources of information, choice of title proper, statements of responsibility, edition, and dates for interactive multimedia works. None of these topics are covered in AACR2R, since that edition does not address interactive multimedia.

4. The guidelines use a GMD not present in AACR2R, since AACR2R does not address interactive multimedia.

5. The guidelines cover a diverse assortment of physical descriptions and related notes either not covered in AACR2R or present only in a scattered way in areas 5 and 7 of various AACR2R chapters.

6. The guidelines provide appendices demonstrating cataloging of interactive multimedia works, including choice of access points, full examples of descriptive cataloging according to the guidelines, MARC tagged examples, and a selected annotated bibliography. AACR2R does not include such material.

- Appendix A summarizes rules for access points, bringing together various concepts in AACR2R as necessary guidance for the cataloger faced with making access points for interactive multimedia. The introduction to Appendix A gives more details.

- Appendices B and C, which present descriptive examples with and without MARC tagging, are intended to illustrate some typical records that result when the guidelines are followed in cataloging interactive multimedia works.

- Appendix D, the Glossary, includes terms which are not present in the AACR2R Glossary. An understanding of the technical vocabulary of interactive multimedia is critical to successful use of the guidelines. It is highly recommended that catalogers read the guidelines Glossary, Appendix D, prior to reading the guidelines.

- Appendix E, a selected annotated bibliography, provides the cataloger with additional assistance in understanding interactive multimedia terms, including selected dictionaries, texts with glossaries, and other resource materials.

The AACR2R areas addressed by the guidelines are area 0 (scope and purpose, definition, additional help, chief source, and prescribed sources of information); area 1 (choice of title proper, general material designation, statements of responsibility); area 2 (edition); area 4 (dates); area 5 (physical description); and area 7 (notes). A brief chart of the areas appears below:

Interactive Multimedia Guidelines	AACR2R Area
A. Scope and purpose	x.0 rules
B. Definition	x.0 rules
C. Additional help for identifying interactive multimedia	x.0 rules
D. Chief source of information	x.0 rules
E. Prescribed sources of information	x.0 rules
F. Choice of title proper	x.1 rules
G. General material designation	x.1 rules
H. Statements of responsibility	x.1 rules
I. Edition	x.2 rules
J. Dates	x.4 rules
K. Physical description	x.5 rules
L. Notes	x.7 rules

Necessarily, practical departures from AACR2R were made in these sections to bring out the critical importance of treating interactive multimedia works as entire entities, while also highlighting the salient nature of the media within. Therefore, there is not always a one-to-one correspondence between the guidelines sections and AACR2R rules, since the guidelines are based on principles found throughout AACR2R, but also serve to answer unique cataloging issues and complications arising from the nature of interactive multimedia works. Extensive consultation with Chapter 9 (Computer Files), Chapter 7 (Motion Pictures and Videorecordings), Chapter 6 (Sound Recordings), Chapter 5 (Music), Chapter 1 (General Rules), and the AACR2R Glossary occurred while the guidelines were being formulated. If there is a conflict between the guidelines and AACR2R when cataloging interactive multimedia works, catalogers should give precedence to the guidelines.

The guidelines are developed for use by the American library community. Their future incorporation into AACR2R is a matter for the Joint Steering Committee for Revision of AACR to initiate and develop.

Parallels Between Microforms and Interactive Multimedia

In AACR2R, instructions on microform materials are given separately, yet the general material designation, [microform], and other specifics of rules for the microform description may be used in conjunction with descriptive cataloging records based in other chapters (e.g., Chapter 2 (Books), Chapter 12 (Serials), Chapter 3 (Cartographic Materials), etc.). An analogous situation may be said to exist for interactive multimedia resources. The general material designation, [interactive multimedia], and other specific instructions for interactive multimedia, lend themselves for use together with instructions found in AACR2R chapters for specific physical carriers (e.g., Chapter 9 (Computer Files); Chapter 7 (Motion Pictures and Videorecordings), etc.).

History and Acknowledgments

Many groups and individuals have had an interest in seeing these guidelines published. Much appreciation and recognition are due all those who have contributed to this challenging endeavor. The following is a brief history of the formal and informal beginnings of this document.

The 1993 Interactive Multimedia Guidelines Review Task Force of the Committee on Cataloging: Description and Access (CC:DA), Cataloging and Classification Section, Association for Library Collections and Technical Services of the American Library Association is responsible for developing and writing the present guidelines. The members and consultants of the Task Force include: Laurel Jizba, Chair, Michigan State University; Eric Childress, Elon College (North Carolina); Nancy Davey, Indianapolis-Marion County Public Library; Josephine F. Davidson, University of Georgia; Sherry Kelley, University of California, Los Angeles; Ann Sandberg-Fox, Saint Michael's College (Vermont); and Joan Swanekamp, Columbia University. A multitude of thanks go to all Task Force members for dedicating considerable wisdom, analytic insight, talent and time to this challenging guidelines project; in addition, Eric Childress, Laurel Jizba and Ann Sandberg-Fox devoted extra hours.

The generous support of the Michigan State University Libraries for this work of the Task Force is gratefully acknowledged. We also want to acknowledge the assistance of John C. Gale, Information Workstation Group, and Philip Dodds, Interactive Multimedia Association, both of whom we consulted repeatedly, along with staff of *The Journal of Educational Multimedia and Hypermedia, The Directory of Multimedia Equipment, Software and Services,* the Multimedia PC Marketing Council, and the Association for Information and Image Management. Elon College served as the listserv host for the Task Force, enabling our work to proceed weekly.

For review of the preliminary final draft, and for comments and suggestions which have confirmed or enhanced the appropriateness and effectiveness of the guidelines, we thank Lowell Ashley, Esther G. Bierbaum, Karen Driessen, Ed Glazier, Richard L. Harwood, Sheila Intner, Craig Locatis, Katha Massey, Glenn Patton, Verna Urbanski, Jay Weitz, and Rebecca Williams.

It is useful to understand the methodologies and timetable used by the 1993 Task Force. First, the ability and willingness of Task Force members to work cooperatively as a team were certainly contributing factors to the Task Force's success in completing the year's work. Besides a team approach, other methodologies employed were continuous weekly communications via electronic mail, fax, or U.S. mail; monthly telephone conference calls; and consultation with experts in interactive multimedia, computers and cataloging throughout the life of the Task Force. The major timetable activities were synthesis and analysis of the over forty comments received orally and three hundred received in writing from catalogers responding to the winter 1992–93 national call for review of the 1992 draft guidelines document; synthesis and analysis of the comments received by June 1993; delivery of interim reports to the annual ALA conference in New Orleans in June 1993; creation of revised draft guidelines by August 1993; development of a national experimental project, with ALA volunteers, using revised guidelines (September 1993); synthesis and analysis of experiment results; revision of the final draft and report to CC:DA.

The September 1993 experimental project was a critical phase in the development of these guidelines. It involved sending five to six surrogate example packets (photocopies of labels, title screens, etc.) from a group of twenty interactive multimedia works, along with revised draft guidelines and a questionnaire, with a request that cataloging be completed within a two-week period. Participants in the experiment were volunteers from the ALA annual conference in New Orleans, June 1993. They were: Lisa Bruere, St. Louis Public Library; Bonnie Dede, University of Michigan; Ian Fairclough, Louisiana State University in Shreveport; Mary Beth Fecko, Rutgers University Libraries; Margaret W. Freed, Norris Medical Library, University of Southern California; Rose Graham, Rice University; Deborah Grimes, University of California, Berkeley; Mary Konkel, University of Akron; Johanne LaGrange, Columbia University; Susan Leister, George Washington University; Joan Lussky, University of Pennsylvania; Brian McCafferty, Wabash College; Bob Mead-Donaldson, Florida International University; Felicia Piscitelli, Texas A. & M. University; Gary J. Rossi, University of California, Irvine; Margaret Shen, Cleveland Public Library; Patricia Thompson, Southwest Texas State University; Patricia Vanderberg, University of California, Berkeley; Patricia VanRyn, Library of Congress; Ellie Wackerman, University of Maryland, College Park; Rebecca Williams, Library of Congress; Charlotte Wolfe, University of Michigan; Gregory Wool, Iowa State University; Dolores Yang, University of Michigan; and Yvonne Wei Zheng, Northwestern University. We are grateful to Pat Thompson for supplying some of the surrogate photocopies for the experimental packets. Thanks go to all of the above for active participation in the 1993 Task Force experiment. Many thanks are also due the forty-some individuals responding in spring 1993 to the guidelines draft. While we cannot name everyone who responded here, we nevertheless appreciate very much the thoughtful comments they shared.

In 1992 an earlier Task Force, the Task Force on Description of Interactive Media, created a CC:DA document which served as the starting point for constructing the present guidelines. That document was written by Ben Tucker, with input from the members and consultants of the 1991–1992 Task Force. Many thanks go to Ben Tucker,

Library of Congress, for chairing the 1991–1992 Task Force. Members of that Task Force were Michael Carpenter, Louisiana State University School of Library and Information Science; Nancy Davey, INCOLSA; Janet Swan Hill, University of Colorado; Laurel Jizba, Michigan State University; and Bruce Chr. Johnson, Library of Congress. Task Force consultants were John Attig, Pennsylvania State University; Karen Driessen, University of Montana; Sheila Intner, Simmons College; Alice Jacobs, National Library of Medicine; Dorian Martyn, Upjohn Corporate Technical Library; Katha D. Massey, University of Georgia; Nancy Olson, Mankato State University; Cecilia Piccolo, Dartmouth College Library; Ann M. Sandberg-Fox, Library of Congress; Sheila Smyth, Nazareth College of Rochester; Verna Urbanski, University of North Florida; Jean Weihs, library consultant; Paul J. Weiss, National Library of Medicine; and Nancy J. Williamson, University of Toronto, Faculty of Library and Information Science.

In June 1991 an organized group of cataloging experts met at the ALA annual meeting in Atlanta to discuss interactive media materials. Sheila Intner, Simmons College, Graduate School of Library and Information Science, deserves much recognition for organizing this initial gathering in Atlanta, for subsequently drafting the first version of the guidelines (November 1991), and for writing the proposal to the Committee on Cataloging: Description and Access (CC:DA) to formally appoint the 1991–1992 Task Force. Participants included most of those named above who were part of the 1991–1992 Task Force, along with others. For the record, the very first informal discussion of interactive multimedia materials took place at a luncheon table at the Online Audiovisual Catalogers' biennial conference in Rochester, New York, October 1990.

On behalf of everyone involved, thanks go to the Committee on Cataloging: Description and Access, the Cataloging and Classification Section, and the Association for Library Collections & Technical Services of the American Library Association, for their willingness to undertake this special project.

> LAUREL JIZBA, *Chair*
> Interactive Multimedia Guidelines Review Task Force
> East Lansing, Michigan, March 1994

CONTENTS

A. Scope and purpose ... 1

B. Definition ... 1

C. Additional help for identifying interactive multimedia ... 2

   1. Does the work use computer technology? ... 2

   2. Does the work offer an appropriate level of user control? ... 2

   3. Does the work offer nonlinear navigation? ... 3

   4. Hardware requirements ... 3

   5. Descriptive words or phrases ... 3

   6. What's not interactive multimedia ... 4

   7. Combinations of separately issued works ... 4

   8. In case of doubt ... 4

   9. Read the Glossary ... 4

D. Chief source of information ... 4

E. Prescribed sources of information ... 6

F. Choice of title proper ... 6

G. General material designation ... 7

H. Statements of responsibility ... 7

I. Edition ... 7

J. Dates ... 8

K. Physical description ... 8

L. Notes ... 10

   System requirements ... 10

   Mode of access ... 11

   Language and script ... 11

   Source of title proper ... 11

   Variations in title ... 11

   General material designation ... 12

   Statements of responsibility ... 12

   Edition and history ... 13

   Physical description ... 13

   Summary ... 14

   Contents ... 14

Appendices

A. Choice of access points ... 15

B. Examples of descriptive cataloging for interactive multimedia works ... 17

C. MARC tagged examples of descriptive cataloging for interactive multimedia works ... 27

D. Glossary ... 36

E. Selected, annotated bibliography of dictionaries, texts and glossaries, and other resource materials on interactive multimedia ... 41

GUIDELINES FOR BIBLIOGRAPHIC DESCRIPTION OF INTERACTIVE MULTIMEDIA

A. Scope and purpose

These are guidelines for the formulation of descriptive cataloging for interactive multimedia as defined in Section B. These guidelines supplement or replace rules for bibliographic description found in the *Anglo-American Cataloguing Rules,* second edition, 1988 revision and the supplementary packet subtitled *Amendments 1993* (jointly identified here as AACR2R). Details of description for interactive multimedia should comply with AACR2R unless compliance would conflict with instructions provided in these guidelines. In case of conflict, prefer the guidelines. Apply relevant rules in Part I of AACR2R for aspects of descriptive cataloging not covered in these guidelines. See the AACR2R rules in Part II (Headings, Uniform Titles, and References) for other aspects of the catalog records being created. In addition, the guidelines' appendices also provide supplementary assistance.

B. Definition

Interactive multimedia: media residing in one or more physical carriers (videodiscs, computer disks, computer optical discs, computer audio discs, etc.) or on computer networks. Interactive multimedia must exhibit both of these characteristics: (1) user-controlled, nonlinear navigation using computer technology; and (2) the combination of two or more media (audio, text, graphics, images, animation, and video) that the user manipulates to control the order and/or nature of the presentation.

1

C. Additional help for identifying interactive multimedia

For additional help in determining whether a work[1] should be cataloged according to these guidelines, consider the following:

> Interactive multimedia may be recorded, published, and/or distributed in a variety of physical carriers (including those which have traditionally been cataloged using AACR2R, Chapters 6, 7, 9, etc.), and/or may be primarily retrievable through computer networks. For the purposes of determining whether or not a work should be cataloged under these guidelines, rather than basing judgment upon the physical carrier(s), consider whether what is being cataloged matches the definition in Section B.

When seeking to determine whether or not a work exhibits the characteristics of "user-controlled, nonlinear navigation using computer technology," consider the following:

1. **Does the work use computer technology?** Although conventional, linear format playback equipment (e.g., a conventional video playback system) may employ computer circuitry and offer some limited ability for users to program its operation (e.g., timer-operated recording), the "computer technology" employed is merely a substitute for electromechanical switches or similar "low-tech" devices. For the purposes of the definition in Section B, do not consider such low-level computerization to represent "using computer technology." Rather, consider whether the item requires a microcomputer, Level III or higher videodisc player, or similarly sophisticated level of computer technology to achieve its design potential. Some online computer network resources may also qualify.

2. **Does the work offer an appropriate level of user control?** The level of user control varies widely among interactive multimedia works and may vary for different users of the same work, depending on the machine environment employed, the knowledge and skill of the user, and other factors. Be aware that user control may range from a modest to a very high level. For

---

1. Interactive multimedia work. In the context of these guidelines, a work of interactive multimedia includes the whole intellectual content, which may be comprised of one or more kinds of entities or a collection or compilation of various entities; this content forms the basis for a single bibliographic description. It does not matter whether or not some parts of the interactive multimedia work have or have not been published or issued at the same time or by the same issuing body, or whether only some of the parts are interactive multimedia.

example, modest user control for interactive videodiscs means the ability to repeat, freeze-frame, and stop the program at chapter codes. A very high level of user control for any type of interactive multimedia work means the ability to break or alter existing links and pathways (and/or create new links and pathways), and to add, delete, and manipulate data.

3. **Does the work offer nonlinear navigation?** This may be difficult to determine at first glance, but a careful reading of descriptive materials for the work or, better still, using the work can be instructive. *Nonlinear navigation* refers to the user's ability to retrieve the information freely or randomly and to move through the content via hyperlinks or similar mechanisms. Nonlinear navigation permits the user to be an active participant in exploring and, in some instances, shaping the content (i.e., creating new paths, choosing among existing paths, repeating sequences, etc., or otherwise manipulating links in a nearly conversational mode between work and user). Usually, no two users will experience the same presentation. Even for the same user, the presentation will probably be different for each interactive multimedia session.

4. **Hardware requirements:** Because interactive multimedia works are available in a variety of physical carriers for various machine environments, hardware requirements information may be helpful in identifying likely candidates for treatment under these guidelines. Look for:

   - words requiring or supporting sound boards (e.g., SoundBlaster, ProMedia, Adlib)

   - display of the MPC (Multimedia PC Marketing Council) or MPC2 logo, or the words *MPC ready, MPC compliant*, etc.

   - presence of trademark logos such as QuickTime or Ultimedia, etc.

   There may also be a requirement for a *multimedia* computer: a required hardware configuration that includes a microcomputer linked to video playback equipment; or a requirement for a Level III, IV, or V videodisc player.

5. **Descriptive words or phrases:** Interactive multimedia works are frequently named or described by the following words or phrases: *interactive media, multimedia, new media, hypermedia, hyper video,* or some variation of these. These phrases are largely, though not entirely, synonymous. While helpful in identifying possible candidates for treatment under these guidelines, the association of multimedia or a similar word or phrase with a work should not be taken as *prima facie* evidence that the work is interactive multimedia. Instead, apply the definition in Section B.

6. **What's not interactive multimedia:** In contrast, the following categories, at least those published prior to 1993, are generally not considered interactive multimedia:

    - textual or graphic applications software programs, such as word processing or computer-assisted design (CAD)

    - computer-assisted instruction (CAI)

    - database management systems

    - graphical user interface systems (GUI)

    - children's books which present text, audio and/or graphics in linear fashion

    - primarily textual databases with some graphics or images

    - video games employing predetermined software paths (even though linear, fixed paths may be hidden from the user)

    Level I and Level II videodiscs *by themselves* do not qualify as interactive multimedia, although they can be a component when control functions are relocated to an external computer with companion software. However, if any of the above meet the criteria in the definition in Section B, then they would qualify as interactive multimedia.

7. **Combinations of separately issued works:** Videodiscs, CD-ROMs, software, etc. issued and cataloged separately (not as interactive multimedia) may, in the future, be combined with each other or new components and reissued by the same or another publisher as *interactive multimedia*. If the Section B definition applies, create a new record, in accordance with cataloging agency standards.

8. **In case of doubt:** If, in the cataloger's judgment, there is doubt after consulting the preceding statements and the examples in these guidelines, do not consider the item to belong to the category *interactive multimedia*. Instead, follow the rules for other types of materials in Part I of AACR2R.

9. **Read the Glossary:** Since an understanding of the technical vocabulary of interactive multimedia is critical to successful use of the guidelines, reading the Glossary prior to reading the guidelines can be very helpful in fostering understanding.

D.   Chief source of information

The chief source of information for interactive multimedia is the entire work. Prefer information that applies to the work as a whole and that includes a collective title. Sources for such information include:

a. Internal sources: information formally presented on the title screen(s) or title frame(s)

b. External sources: labels permanently affixed to the carrier

container (e.g., box) issued by the publisher or manufacturer

accompanying textual materials (printed or online)[2]

In case of variation in fullness of the information, prefer the source with the most complete information.

If the information is not available from the sources listed above, take it from the following sources (in this order of preference):

Other published descriptions of the work

Other sources (e.g., publisher's brochures)

Always give the source of the title proper in a note.

Example (when chief source information is not available for the whole work):

The original container is missing and the internal sources do not provide comprehensive bibliographic information for the whole work, the three possible chief sources then are the following:

Computer disk label title   =   *AIDS, an adult educational program*

[plus information about 1994 issue of disk and its publisher]

Videodisc label title   =   *AIDS information program*

[plus additional information about version of videodisc, its 1993 copyright, and the one creator associated with it]

User's guide title   =   *Acquired immune deficiency syndrome: an adult education program*

[plus additional information about all creators, version, 1994 copyright, publishers, etc., for whole item]

---

2. Within the context of these guidelines, accompanying textual materials (printed or online) are considered to be an integral part of the whole interactive multimedia work and of the chief source of information.

In this example, note that labels on the Videodisc and on the Computer disk are in part specific to these physical carriers (the one creator applicable to the Videodisc; the information about a later version of the Computer disk). In contrast, the information on the User's guide is comprehensive in applying to the whole of all items together by giving all the names in its statement of responsibility. Select the User's guide as the chief source of information for this example.

E. Prescribed sources of information

The prescribed source(s) of information for each area of the description for interactive multimedia is as follows:

Title and statement of responsibility area	Chief source
Edition	Chief source
Publication, distribution, etc.	Chief source
Physical description	Any source (e.g., chief source, other published descriptions of the work, other sources)
Series	Chief source
Note	Any source (e.g., chief source, other published descriptions of the work, other sources)
Standard number and terms of availability	Any source (e.g., chief source, other published descriptions of the work, other sources)

F. Choice of title proper

According to the preceding guidelines, the most comprehensive source chosen as the chief source must include a title for the whole work. When this title varies in the chief source (i.e., there is more than one expression of the title on the container(s), internal label(s), other physical carrier(s)), select the fullest title as the title proper, if such a comparison is possible. Otherwise, the cataloger must use judgment in selecting as the title proper the best expression of the title. For example, if a container for an interactive multimedia videodisc is chosen as the chief source, and it shows the comprehensive title in two forms: "ChemSci II videodisc," and "ChemSci II videodisc database 2000," choose as the title proper "ChemSci II videodisc database 2000."

Always give the source of the title proper in a note.

G. General material designation

Use as the general material designation [GMD]: [interactive multimedia]

> Compton's multimedia encyclopedia [interactive multimedia]
>
> From Alice to ocean [interactive multimedia]
>
> Desert Storm [interactive multimedia]

N.B. The GMD [interactive multimedia] has been specially formulated for use *only* within the context of these guidelines.

H. Statements of responsibility

Transcribe statements of responsibility relating to those persons or bodies responsible for the entire content of the interactive multimedia work (e.g., interactive multimedia developers, authors, designers, or others similarly named as having principal or equally shared responsibility for the creation of the whole interactive multimedia work). If the statements of responsibility are lengthy, give them in a note.

> All my hummingbirds have alibis [interactive multimedia] / composer, project director, Morton Sobotnick
>
> Richard Scarry's best neighborhood disc ever! [interactive multimedia] / produced by Phillips Interactive Media of America in association with Richard Scarry
>
> Communism and the cold war [interactive multimedia] / ABC-News Interactive ; created and developed as a joint project with the Department of Education, State of Florida

Give all other statements of responsibility, including those confined to the creation of specific parts of the interactive multimedia work in a note: musical or visual performers, ensembles, video graphic designers, guidebook editors, applications programmers, choreographers, narrators, script writers, costumers, set designers, sponsors for a specific part of a work, etc., if they are considered important for a particular catalog or bibliographic agency.

I. Edition

Transcribe a statement or statements relating to an edition of the interactive multimedia work as a whole. In case of doubt about whether the statement or statements apply to the work as a whole, do not record the statement(s) in the edition area.

Rather, record a doubtful statement or statements applying to the whole work in a note.

> Version 3.1A
>
> 1993 version, Macintosh

If there are multiple edition statements relating to parts or pieces of the work, give each statement in a note.

> Ed. statement on videodisc label: Interactive ed.
>
> Ed. statement on computer disk label: Version 3.1.2

Always give the source of the edition statement in a note.

> Ed. statement from container
>
> Ed. statement from guide and computer disk label

J. Dates

Use the latest date, wherever it can be located. There may be multiple dates that apply to various aspects of the work (including copyright, distribution, release, and publication). Treat all of the dates as applying to the whole work, and consider whichever date is the latest to be the most indicative of the most recent manifestation of the whole work. The copyright date is the most typical date type seen on interactive multimedia items. Multiple dates are very common, particularly copyright dates. Given the following, a catalog record would have the date: c1993.

c1990 Harper Collins	*(booklet in CD-ROM container)*
First printing 1992, c1993	*(reference card)*
1991, copyright 1992, 1993 by Apple Computer, Inc.	*(user's guide book, t.p. verso)*
c1991–93 T & H Software	*(HyperCard stack disc label)*
c1989 Graphics by Artware Corp.	*(title screen, CD-ROM)*
c1991 Sound by VoiceMaster, Inc.	*(title screen, CD-ROM)*

Give a note on discrepancies in dates, if judged bibliographically significant.

K. Physical description

For the specific material designation, give the term found in the appropriate x.5B (extent of item) rule of Part I of AACR2R; if the term is inadequate or inappropriate, give as the term the specific name of the part as concisely as possible, (e.g., *1 disk* or *1 disc*).

For any cataloger-formulated statement under these guidelines, use *disc* for any computer optical disc (e.g., CD-ROM) or computer magneto-optical disc, and use *disk* for any magnetic computer disk. Note that the two spellings, *disc* and *disk,* provide results somewhat at variance with examples in AACR2R.

If the interactive multimedia work is made up of multiple physical carriers, apply 1.10C2 of AACR2R, using either method (a) or method (b). Method (a) of 1.10C2 groups all physical descriptions together. Method (b) of 1.10C2 gives separate physical descriptions for each distinct class of material.

The following are examples of physical descriptions for interactive multimedia works made up of several types of material, applying method (a) and method (b) of 1.10C2:

Method (a) of 1.10C2

1 videodisc, 3 computer disks (3 1/2 in.), 1 connector cable, 1 guide, 2 folded wall maps, 1 poster

Method (b) of 1.10C2

> 1 videodisc : sd., col. ; 12 in.
>
> 4 computer disks ; 3 1/2 in.
>
> 1 table of contents/user's manual (104 p.) ; 28 cm.
>
> 1 barcodes book (154 p.) ; 28 cm.

If the interactive multimedia work is made up of a single physical carrier, apply the provisions for physical description as found in the applicable chapter of Part I of AACR2R, rules x.5 (e.g., for sound discs, see Chapter 6; videodiscs, Chapter 7; computer disks and computer optical discs, Chapter 9).

The following is an example of a physical description for an interactive multimedia work made up of one physical carrier:

> 1 computer optical disc : sd., col. ; 4 3/4 in. + 1 booklet + 1 user guide

Do not use method (c) of 1.10C2 (i.e., use of a general term, such as *pieces* to cover all parts), since works of interactive multimedia may be made up of identifiable materials (videodiscs, compact discs, computer disks, manuals, etc.) which must be named specifically so that playback system requirements may be determined (among other reasons).

As with computer files (cf. Chapter 9 of AACR2R), a physical description is not provided for a work of interactive multimedia that is available only by remote access.

L.   Notes

Notes are optional unless otherwise stated. In accordance with AACR2R rules 0.7 and 0.9, exercise judgement, as determined by the cataloging policy for a particular catalog or bibliographic agency.

System requirements

Make a system requirements note if there is only one physical carrier. If there are multiple physical carriers, make either one system requirements note or multiple systems requirements notes; follow either method (a) or method (b) below. Begin the system requirements note(s) with System requirements:. Give the following characteristics in the order in which they are listed below. Precede each characteristic, other than the first, by a semicolon.

> the make and model of the computer(s) or videodisc player on which the file(s) are designed to run
>
> the amount of computer memory required
>
> the name of the operating system
>
> the software requirements (including the programming language)
>
> the kind and characteristics of any required or recommended peripherals

Either group system requirements for multiple carriers together, using method (a), as in the following three examples:

Method (a) for system requirements

> System requirements: Macintosh computer; Apple System software (version 6.0.5 or more); HyperCard (version 1.0 or later); hard disk drive; videodisc player (Pioneer 2200, 4200, 6000A, 6010A, 8000); RS232 cable connector (from Macintosh to videodisc player)

> ———

> System requirements: Phillips interactive compact disc (CD-I) player with monitor

> ———

> System requirements: UNIX workstation with Mosaic applications program

Or, alternatively, to highlight distinctive system features for multiple carriers, apply method (b), as in the following example:

Method (b) for system requirements

System requirements: Macintosh computer: Apple System software (version 6.0.5 or more); HyperCard (version 1.0 or later); hard disk drive

System requirements: Videodisc player (Pioneer 2200, 4200, 6000A, 6010A, 8000); RS232 cable connector (from Macintosh to videodisc player)

Mode of access

If an interactive multimedia work is only available by remote access, always specify the mode of access.

Mode of access: Internet and World-Wide Web

Mode of access: Internet. Host: quake.think.com

Language and script

Spoken and written instruction in English and French (CD-ROM, disks 1-2, guide 1)

Closed-captioned for the hearing impaired

Source of title proper

Always give in a note the source of the title proper.

Title from videodisc title screen

Title from computer optical disc label

Title from videodisc label

Title from videodisc container

Title from computer disk label

Title from computer disk container

Title from user guide

Title from magneto-optical disc manual

Variations in title

Make notes on variations in title, particularly if an added entry is justified under title differences described in rule 21.2.

Title on videodisc label [vol 1]: The dream machine laserguide

Title on videodisc label [vol. 2]: Dream machine : the visual computer

Title on computer optical disc label: The magic flute

Title on guidebook cover: Orsay videodisc

File name: CC.BIOLOGY.INTERMED

General material designation

AACR2R considers GMD optional: if the GMD [interactive multimedia] is not used (and the cataloger has determined it is an interactive multimedia work), make a note indicating the work is interactive multimedia, or include the words *interactive multimedia* in a summary note (per x.7B17 of AACR2R).

Statements of responsibility

Make a note for lengthy statements of responsibility relating to the entire interactive multimedia work, if important in the cataloger's judgement. For other statements of responsibility, including those confined to the creation of specific parts of the interactive multimedia work, make notes such as, for example: musical or visual performers, ensembles, video graphic designers, guidebook editors, applications programmers, choreographers, narrators, script writers, costumers, set designers, sponsors for one part of a work, etc., if considered important for a particular catalog or bibliographic agency.

Follow rules in 7.7 for motion pictures and videorecording performances if featured as part of an interactive multimedia work, if considered important for a particular catalog or bibliographic agency. Also, optionally, follow 6.7B6 for sound recordings which may be featured as part of an interactive multimedia title, if important in the cataloger's judgement.

Analysis and musicology by Irene Girton

Program design by Robert Winter and Robert Stein

Programming, Tom Greene

Correspondents, Barrie Dunsmore, Carol Simpson ; with Ted Koppel

Producer, Mary Ann Norris ; graphic design, Danielle Eubank ; programming, Steve Riggins ; audio editor, Michael Schwartz ; documentation, Moira Waddell ; editorial, Peter Bogdanoff ; executive producer, Suzanne Escoffier

Photography, Betty Freeman . . . [et al.] ; text editor, Jo Ann Baldinger ; art direction, Jim Wood, Brian Speight

Elizabeth Leonskaja, piano ; Alan Berg Quartett

Busch Quartett (1st-3rd works) ; Adolf Busch, violin, Rudolph Serkin, piano (4th-5th works)

Credits: Video production, Wolfgang Mohr ; producer, Hermut Muhle

Cast: Matti Salminen (Sarastro), Hans-Peter Blochwitz (Tamino), Barbara Bonney (Pamina), Edita Gruberova (Queen of the Night), Anton Scharinger (Papageno), Edith Schmid (Papagena) ; Zurich Opera House Chorus ; Zurich Opera House Orchestra

Edition and history

Ed. statement from guide and computer disk label

Originally issued as Level II videorecording

User guide dated 1990

Sound by VoiceMaster, Inc. copyright 1991

Compact audio disc previously released by Teldec Records p1989

"Audio notes" first published 1985

Includes excerpts from the 1979 videorecording

"A full digital recording (DDD) of the performance recorded Mar. 1985 in Berlin, Germany and released on Teldec 35766"

"Multimedia Master version of the original 1985 two videodisc version"

Physical description

Make notes on important physical details that are not included in the physical description area, especially if these affect the use of the work.

In two containers

Analog recording   *(for digital disc made from analog recording)*

Digital and analog tracks both in English and German

Digital recording of the music

Summary

Give a brief objective summary of the content of an interactive multimedia work unless another part of the description provides enough information.

Summary: Includes more than 7,000 still images, 400 diagrams, dozens of motion pictures and 3D computer graphics, selected to support standard biology texts and lecture subjects. The image directory and software collection allow students and teachers to locate and identify images by common name, scientific name or classification; produce reusable custom slide or video shows; write interactive lessons and create presentations and interactive reports.

—

Summary: Animated sequences feature characters like Huckle the Cat and Mr. Fumble. Children choose places and friends in Busytown to visit, such as the fire station, flower shop, etc. In the process they practice pre-reading skills, learn to count, recognize patterns, build memory skills and develop vocabulary.

—

Summary: Combines the interactivity of HyperCard with a compact audio disc to explore Mozart's music, including the biographical and historical circumstances of its creation, using text, graphics and audio examples.

—

Summary: Musicological analysis and HyperCard applications give users an in-depth experience of Mozart's comic opera, in which Prince Tamino and birdcatcher Papageno enter the magic realm of the Queen of the Night. Both find true love after an arduous search for truth.

—

Summary: Noted music critic Alan Rich sweeps through the musical panorama from surviving fragments of Greek chant to the complexities of 18th century Bach, with profuse illustrations, art works, musical examples, a musical and cultural glossary, and a collector's guide to compact discs featuring Rich's favorite recorded performances. Musical examples are linked to the Catalog of recordings; HyperCard enables users to add their own notes to both the Essay and Catalog sections

Contents

List the individually named parts of an interactive multimedia work.

Contents: Data (3:00) — 5 scenes from an imaginary ballet (10:31) — MIDI and interactor / Mark Coniglio (3:29) — The recording / Michael Hoenig (3:35) — A composer's views (13:22) — All my hummingbirds have alibis (28:47).

Make notes on additional or partial contents when appropriate.

CHOICE OF ACCESS POINTS

This appendix is intended to give guidance to the cataloger in the making of access points for interactive multimedia works. Apply relevant rules in Part II of AACR2. However, since interactive multimedia works may incorporate other kinds of works, each with their own statements of responsibility, the complex relationships interactive multimedia works present in determining appropriate access points may not be immediately evident to the cataloger. It is also the case that often, but not always, the interactive multimedia work may, in the end, have a main entry under title. Added entries may be made case by case per instructions in AACR2, rules 21.29 and 21.30. See Appendix B for some examples illustrating choice of access points, as well as description. It is always the option of the cataloger to exercise judgment, as determined by the cataloging policy for a particular catalog or bibliographic agency, in choosing access points.

Principal responsibility for the whole interactive multimedia work

Make access points for those persons or bodies responsible for the entire content of the interactive multimedia work (e.g., interactive multimedia developers, authors, designers, or others similarly named as having principal or equally shared responsibility for the creation of the whole interactive multimedia work). Follow rules in Part II, AACR2R, in determining main entry. Make added entries according to the instructions in AACR2R, rules 21.29 and 21.30.

Mixed responsibility for the whole interactive multimedia work

If responsibility is shared among more than three persons or corporate bodies for the entire content of the interactive multimedia work, and principal responsibility is not attributed to any one, two, or three, enter under title. Make added entries according to the instructions in AACR2R, 21.29 and 21.30.

Responsibility for specific parts of an interactive multimedia work

If responsibility is confined to the creation of specific parts of the interactive multimedia work (e.g., musical or visual performers, ensembles, video graphic designers, guidebook editors, applications programmers, choreographers, narrators, script writers, costumers, set designers, sponsors for one part of a work, etc.), make added entries if they are considered important for a particular catalog or bibliographic agency. Make added entries according to the instructions in AACR2R, 21.29 and 21.30. In case of conflict with instructions provided in AACR2R and these guidelines, prefer the guidelines.

EXAMPLES OF DESCRIPTIVE CATALOGING FOR INTERACTIVE MULTIMEDIA WORKS

These examples are intended to show full descriptive cataloging when cataloging has been completed using the Guidelines for Bibliographic Description of Interactive Multimedia *in conjunction with AACR2R. Specifically illustrated sections of the guidelines are noted before each example. Other descriptive portions in the examples are based on descriptive rules in AACR2R, but specific AACR2R rules have not been cited. Suggestions for access points are also given.*

EXAMPLE A: Planetary manager.

This example illustrates these guidelines sections:

F. *Choice of title proper*

G. *GMD*

I. *Edition*

J. *Dates*

K. *Physical description (method (a) of 1.10C2)*

L. *Notes for system requirements, source of title proper, variations in title, statements of responsibility, multiple edition statements relating to part of the interactive multimedia work, source of edition statement, physical description, summary note.*

Other descriptive portions are based on descriptive rules in AACR2R.

EXAMPLE A: Planetary manager.

Planetary manager [interactive multimedia]. — IBM linkway version. — Washington, D.C. : National Geographic Society, c1992.

1 videodisc, 3 computer disks (3 1/2 in.), 1 connector cable, 1 guide, 2 folded wall maps, 1 poster. — (GTV)

System requirements for Turbo GTV configuration (interactive video): IBM PS/2 computer (Model 25 286 or Model 30 286 or better) with 1MB RAM, DOS 3.3 or higher, 3 1/2 in. disk drive, hard disk drive, VGA graphics, mouse, printer (optional); videodisc player (Pioneer LD-V2200, 4200, 6000, 6000A, 6010, 8000 or Sony LDP-1200, 1500, 1550, or MDP-1100), with TV or monitor, audio cable, and video cable.

Title from guide.

Also called GTV planetary manager.

Created and developed as a joint project of the Florida State Dept. of Education ; videodisc produced with Colossal Pictures ; computer software and interface design by LucasArts Learning.

Ed. statement on computer disks: Version 1.0.

Videodisc also issued in "Standard GTV" configuration without computer disks or in "Deluxe GTV" configuration with bar codes.

Ed. statement from guide.

Summary: An interactive video that explores the state of the earth. Students cast as "planetary managers" examine environmental problems, explore the consequences, and wrestle with solutions. Students are also able to create customized presentations using the still and moving images they find on the videodisc.

ISBN 0-7922-2048-X (guide)

....

Access points: National Geographic Society (U.S.)
                          Florida Department of Education
                          Colossal Pictures (Firm)   *(if considered important)*
                          LucasArts Learning   *(if considered important)*
                          GTV planetary manager   *(variant title)*

EXAMPLE B: Biology encyclopedia.

This example illustrates these guidelines sections:

F. *Choice of title proper*

G. GMD

H. *Statements of responsibility*

J. *Dates*

K. *Physical description (method (b) of 1.10C2)*

L. *Notes for system requirements, source of title proper, variations in title, statements of responsibility, credits, physical description, summary note.*

Other descriptive portions are based on descriptive rules in AACR2R.

EXAMPLE B: Biology encyclopedia.

Biology encyclopedia [interactive multimedia] / Harper Collins. — New York, NY : HarperCollins, c1991.
    1 videodisc : sd., col. ; 12 in.
    4 computer disks ; 3 1/2 in.
    1 table of contents/user's manual (104 p.) ; 28 cm.
    1 barcodes book (154 p.) ; 28 cm.

    System requirements for videodisc (Level I): Videodisc player that reads chapter codes and picture stops, television receiver or monitor; audio and video cables, or an RF cable.
    System requirements for computer disks (Level III): Macintosh Plus or later; HyperCard 1.2.2 or later; hard disk with enough free space for the stack (3MBytes); HD backup; videodisc player with serial port (such as Pioneer 2200, 4200, 8000, 6000 series; Sony 1200, 1500, 2000; or Hitachi 9500, or other players that use the same commands); cable to connect the Macintosh modem to the videodisc player.
    Title from videodisc label.
    Title on computer disk labels: BioPedia HyperCard stack.
    "A production of Nebraska Interactive Video, Inc. for Harper, Collins [sic] and Carolina Biological Supply Company"—User's manual.
    Credits: Content developed by Charles Lytle and William Surver ; videodisc and HyperCard stack design by J. Mark Turner ; HyperCard stack programming by Helen Brooks.
    Two-sided CAV laser videodisc that can be used as Level I without the computer or as Level III with the computer.
    Summary: An interactive biology encyclopedia with a videodisc containing 31 content chapters, more than 1500 photographic slides, over 1000 illustrations, and over 50 minutes of motion video. The HyperCard stack allows the user to access information on the videodisc.
    ISBN 0-673-16331-1

• •

Access points: Persons listed in Credits note   *(if considered important)*
                          HarperCollins
                          Nebraska Interactive Video, Inc.
                          Carolina Biological Supply Company
                          BioPedia HyperCard stack   *(title of computer disks)*

EXAMPLE C: The enduring vision.

This example illustrates these guidelines sections:

F. *Choice of title proper*

G. GMD

H. *Statements of responsibility*

I. *Edition*

J. *Dates*

K. *Physical description (when the interactive multi-media work is made up of a single physical carrier)*

L. *Notes for system requirements, source of title proper, credits, multiple edition statements relating to part of the interactive multimedia work, edition and history, source of edition statement, physical description, summary note.*

Other descriptive portions are based on descriptive rules in AACR2R.

EXAMPLE C: The enduring vision.

   The enduring vision [interactive multimedia] : a history of the American people / Boyer . . .
[et al.] ; developed by Bryten, Inc. — Interactive ed., 1993 version. — Lexington, Mass. : D.C.
Heath, c1993.
   1 computer optical disc : sd., col. ; 4 3/4 in. + 1 booklet + 1 user guide

   System requirements: Macintosh LC or II series; 4MB RAM; System 6.0.7 or higher;
QuickTime 1.5 or higher; hard disk with at least 2MB available; 13 in. color monitor;
CD-ROM drive.
   Title from container.
   Credits: Project manager, Brian Maguire ; developmental editor, Laura Senier.
   Ed. statement on user guide: 1993 version, Macintosh version.
   Electronic version of The enduring vision, 2nd ed.
   Ed. statement from container.
   "This CD-ROM disc may only be played in a CD-ROM drive. It is not designed to play in
an audio CD device or other CD players"—Booklet.
   Summary: An interactive American history textbook supplemented with photographs and
illustrations, graphs and maps (many animated to depict change over time), and live video
segments. Includes primary source documents, a notebook for user annotations, chronologies,
glossaries, bibliographies, and self-tests.
   ISBN 0-669-32461-2

....

Access points: Paul S. Boyer
                             Bryten, Inc.
                             D.C. Heath and Company
                             Enduring vision   *(uniform title added entry for the textbook)*

EXAMPLE D: String quartet in C major, K. 465 [interactive multimedia].

This example illustrates these guidelines sections:

    F. Choice of title proper

    G. GMD

    H. Statements of responsibility

    J. Dates

    K. Physical description (method (a) of 1.10C2)

    L. Notes for system requirements, source of title proper, production credits, important physical details not included in the physical description area, summary note.

Other descriptive portions are based on descriptive rules in AACR2R.

EXAMPLE D: String quartet in C major, K. 465 [interactive multimedia].

String quartet in C major, K. 465 [interactive multimedia] : the "dissonant" /
Mozart ; performed by Angeles Quartet ; program by Robert Winter. — Santa Monica, CA :
Voyager Co., c1991.
    1 computer laser optical disc : sd. ; 4 3/4 in. + 1 user's guide (7 p. ; 22 cm.) — (Voyager
companion series)

    System requirements: Macintosh computer; Apple System software version 6.0.7 or higher;
HyperCard software version 2.1 or higher with HyperCard 2.0 fonts; hard disk drive;
Macintosh-compatible CD-ROM drive with headphones or speakers, and CD-ROM drivers
installed in System folder.
    Title from disc label.
    Production credits: Director, David Miller ; producers, Peter Bogdanoff, Wendy Bricht.
    Digital recording of the music.
    Summary: Combines the interactivity of HyperCard with a compact audio disc to explore
Mozart's music, including the biographical and historical circumstances of its creation, using
text, graphics and audio examples.
    "CDAC-012800"
    ISBN 1-555940-217-2

....

Access points: Mozart, Wolfgang Amadeus, $d 1756-1791
                        Winter, Robert, $d 1945-
                        Author- uniform title entry for Mozart and his String quartet
                          in C major, K. 465
                        Angeles Quartet
                        Voyager Company
                        Dissonant   *(variant title)*

MARC TAGGED EXAMPLES
OF DESCRIPTIVE CATALOGING
FOR INTERACTIVE MULTIMEDIA WORKS

These examples are intended to give guidance in assigning MARC tags to the full descriptive cataloging in Appendix B, after cataloging has been completed using the Guidelines for Bibliographic Description of Interactive Multimedia *in conjunction with AACR2R. Examples A and B,* Planetary manager *and* Biology encyclopedia, *are given to illustrate tagged records following RLG input standards for the Research Libraries Network (RLIN). Examples C and D,* The enduring vision *and* String quartet in C major, K. 465, *are given to illustrate tagged records following input standards for the OCLC network. MARC tagging is indicated for records to be created in these networks before implementation of MARC format integration; notes indicate appropriate tags after MARC format integration (for variable field tags only; leader encoding cannot be fully predicted at this time).*

MARC TAGGED EXAMPLE A

Planetary manager following RLG input standards for RLIN (not a complete record).[a] (Prior to MARC format integration implementation).

This example illustrates these guidelines sections:

F. *Choice of title proper*

G. *GMD*

I. *Edition*

J. *Dates*

K. *Physical description (method (a) of 1.10C2)*

L. *Notes for system requirements, source of title proper, variations in title, statements of responsibility, multiple edition statements relating to part of the interactive multimedia work, source of edition statement, physical description, summary note.*

Other descriptive portions are based on descriptive rules in AACR2R.

MARC TAGGED EXAMPLE A

Planetary manager following RLG input standards for RLIN (not a complete record).[a] (Prior to MARC format integration implementation).

ID : CRLG94-DO		RTYP : c	ST : d	FRN :	MS:	EL: 1 AD:01-07-94
CC : 9114	BLT : mm	DCF : a	CSD : d	MOD :	SNR :	ATC : UD:01-07-94
CP : dcu	L : eng	GPC :	FRQ : n	REG :	TMDF : z	AUD :
PC : c	PD : 1992/		PSC :	D :		

020[b]   079222048X$c(guide)

245 00 Planetary manager$h[interactive multimedia]

250   IBM linkway version.

260   Washington, D.C. :$bNational Geographic Society,$cc1992.

300   1 videodisc, 3 computer disks (3 1/2 in.), 1 connector cable, 1 guide, 2 folded wall maps, 1 poster.

440 0 GTV

538   System requirements for Turbo GTV configuration (interactive video): IBM PS/2 computer (Model 25 286 or Model 30 286 or better) with 1MB RAM, DOS 3.3 or higher, 3 1/2 in. disk drive, hard disk drive, VGA graphics, mouse, printer (optional); videodisc player (Pioneer LD-V2200, 4200, 6000, 6000A, 6010, 8000 or Sony LDP-1200, 1500, 1550, or MDP-1100), with TV or monitor, audio cable, and video cable.

500   Title from guide.

500   Also called GTV planetary manager.

500   Created and developed as a joint project of the Florida State Dept. of Education ; videodisc produced with Colossal Pictures ; computer software and interface design by LucasArts Learning.

500   Ed. statement on computer disks: Version 1.0.

500   Videodisc also issued in "Standard GTV" configuration without computer disks or in "Deluxe GTV" configuration with bar codes.

500   Ed. statement from guide.

520[b]   An interactive video that explores the state of the earth. Students cast as "planetary managers" examine environmental problems, explore the consequences, and wrestle with solutions. Students are also able to create customized presentations using the still and moving images they find on the videodisc.

....

Access points:

710 20 National Geographic Society (U.S.)

710 10 Florida. $b Department of Education

710 20 Colossal Pictures (Firm)   *(if considered important)*

710 20 LucasArts Learning   *(if considered important)*

740 01 GTV planetary manager   *(variant title)*

---

[a] All subject work and several 0xx fields have been omitted from this record.

[b] The 020 and 520 are tagged with the understanding that display and print constants for national and local bibliographic systems have been taken into account.

MARC TAGGED EXAMPLE B

Biology encyclopedia following RLG input standards for RLIN (not a complete record).[a] (Prior to MARC format integration implementation).

This example illustrates these guidelines sections:

F. *Choice of title proper*

G. GMD

H. *Statements of responsibility*

J. *Dates*

K. *Physical description (method (b) of 1.10C2)*

L. *Notes for system requirements, source of title proper, variations in title, statements of responsibility, credits, physical description, summary note.*

Other descriptive portions are based on descriptive rules in AACR2R.

MARC TAGGED EXAMPLE B

Biology encyclopedia following RLG input standards for RLIN (not a complete record).[a] (Prior to MARC format integration implementation).

ID : CRLG94-D1   RTYP : c   ST : d   FRN :   MS: EL: 1 AD:01-07-94
CC : 9114   BLT : mm   DCF : a   CSD : d   MOD :   SNR :   ATC : UD:01-07-94
CP : dcu   L : eng   GPC :   FRQ : n   REG :   TMDF : z   AUD :
PC : c   PD : 1991/   PSC :   D :

020[b]   0673163311
245 00 Biology encyclopedia$h[interactive multimedia] /$cHarper Collins.
260 00 New York, NY :$bHarperCollins,$cc1991.
300   1 videodisc :$b sd., col. ;$c 12 in.
300   4 computer disks ;$c 3 1/2 in.
300   1 table of contents/user's manual (104 p.) ;$c 28 cm.
300   1 barcodes book (154 p.) ;$c 28 cm.
538   System requirements for videodisc (Level I): Videodisc player that reads chapter codes and picture stops, television receiver or monitor; audio and video cables, or an RF cable.
538   System requirements for computer disks (Level III): Macintosh Plus or later; HyperCard 1.2.2 or later; hard disk with enough free space for the stack (3MBytes); HD backup; videodisc player with serial port (such as Pioneer 2200, 4200, 8000, 6000 series; Sony 1200, 1500, 2000; or Hitachi 9500, or other players that use the same commands); cable to connect the Macintosh modem to the videodisc player.
500   Title from videodisc label.
500   Title on computer disk labels: BioPedia HyperCard stack.
500   "A production of Nebraska Interactive Video, Inc. for Harper, Collins [sic] and Carolina Biological Supply Company"—User's manual.
500[c]   Credits: Content developed by Charles Lytle and William Surver ; videodisc and HyperCard stack design by J. Mark Turner ; HyperCard stack programming by Helen Brooks.
500   Two-sided CAV laser videodisc that can be used as Level I without the computer or as Level III with the computer.
520[b]   An interactive biology encyclopedia with a videodisc containing 31 content chapters, more than 1500 photographic slides, over 1000 illustrations, and over 50 minutes of motion video. The HyperCard stack allows the user to access information on the videodisc.

• •

Access points: 700 xx Persons listed in Credits note   *(if considered important)*
                            710 20 HarperCollins
                            710 20 Nebraska Interactive Video, Inc.
                            710 20 Carolina Biological Supply Company
                            740 01 BioPedia HyperCard stack   *(title of computer disks)*

---

[a] All subject work and several 0xx fields have been omitted from this record.

[b] The 020 and 520 are tagged with the understanding that display and print constants for national and local bibliographic systems have been taken into account.

[c] After MARC format integration this "Credits:" note would be tagged 508.

MARC TAGGED EXAMPLE C

The enduring vision following input standards for the OCLC network (not a complete record).[a] (Prior to MARC format integration implementation).

> *This example illustrates these guidelines sections:*
>
> F. *Choice of title proper*
>
> G. GMD
>
> H. *Statements of responsibility*
>
> I. *Edition*
>
> J. *Dates*
>
> K. *Physical description (when the interactive multimedia work is made up of a single physical carrier)*
>
> L. *Notes for system requirements, source of title proper, credits, multiple edition statements relating to part of the interactive multimedia work, edition and history, source of edition statement, physical description, summary note.*
>
> *Other descriptive portions are based on descriptive rules in AACR2R.*

MARC TAGGED EXAMPLE C

The enduring vision following input standards for the OCLC network (not a complete record).[a] (Prior to MARC format integration implementation).

OCLC:xxxxxxxx   Rec stat: n

Entered:	19940110	Replaced:	19940110	Used:19940110
Type: m	Bibl lvl: m	Source: d	Lang: eng	
File: m	Enc lvl: I	Govt Pub:	Ctry: mau	
Audience:	Mod rec:	Frequen: n	Regulr:	
Desc: a		Pub st: c	Dates: 1993	

245 04 The enduring vision $h [interactive multimedia] : $b a history of the American people / $c Boyer . . . [et al.] ; developed by Bryten, Inc.

250   Interactive ed., 1993 version.

260   Lexington, Mass. : $b D.C. Heath, $c c1993.

300   1 computer optical disc : $b sd., col. ; $c 4 3/4 in. + $e 1 booklet + 1 user guide

538   System requirements: Macintosh LC or II series; 4MB RAM; System 6.0.7 or higher; QuickTime 1.5 or higher; hard disk with at least 2MB available; 13 in. color monitor; CD-ROM drive.

500   Title from container.

500[b]   Credits: Project manager, Brian Maguire ; developmental editor, Laura Senier.

500   Ed. statement on user guide: 1993 version, Macintosh version.

500   Electronic version of The enduring vision, 2nd ed.

500   Ed. statement from container.

500   "This CD-ROM disc may only be played in a CD-ROM drive. It is not designed to play in an audio CD device or other CD players"—Booklet.

520[c]   An interactive American history textbook supplemented with photographs and illustrations, graphs and maps (many animated to depict change over time), and live video segments. Includes primary source documents, a notebook for user annotations, chronologies, glossaries, bibliographies, and self-tests.

020[c]   0669324612

. . . .

Access points: 700 10 Boyer, Paul S.

710 20 Bryten, Inc.

710 20 D.C. Heath and Company

740 01 Enduring vision   *(uniform title added entry for the textbook)*

---

[a] All subject work and several 0xx fields have been omitted from this record.

[b] After MARC format integration this "Credits:" note would be tagged 508.

[c] The 020 and 520 are tagged with the understanding that display and print constants for national and local bibliographic systems have been taken into account.

MARC TAGGED EXAMPLE D

String quartet in C major, K. 465 following input standards for the OCLC network (not a complete record).[a] (Prior to MARC format integration implementation).

This example illustrates these guidelines sections:

F. *Choice of title proper*
G. *GMD*
H. *Statements of responsibility*
J. *Dates*
K. *Physical description (method (a) of 1.10C2)*
L. *Notes for system requirements, source of title proper, production credits, important physical details not included in the physical description area, summary note.*

Other descriptive portions are based on descriptive rules in AACR2R.

MARC TAGGED EXAMPLE D

String quartet in C major, K. 465 following input standards for the OCLC network (not a complete record).[a] (Prior to MARC format integration implementation).

OCLC:xxxxxxxx   Rec stat: n

Entered:	19940110	Replaced:	19940110 Used:19940110
Type: m	Bibl lvl: m	Source: d	Lang: eng
File: m	Enc lvl: I	Govt Pub:	Ctry: cau
Audience:	Mod rec:	Frequen:	Regulr:
Desc: a		Pub st: c	Dates: 1991

245 10 String quartet in C major, K. 465 $h [interactive multimedia] : $b the "dissonant" / $c Mozart ; performed by Angeles Quartet ; program by Robert Winter.

260   Santa Monica, CA : $b Voyager Co., $c c1991.

300   1 computer laser optical disc : $c sd., 4 3/4 in. + $e 1 user's guide (7 p. ; 22 cm.)

440 0   Voyager companion series

538   System requirements: Macintosh computer; Apple System software version 6.0.7 or higher; HyperCard software version 2.1 or higher with HyperCard 2.0 fonts; hard disk drive; Macintosh-compatible CD-ROM drive with headphones or speakers, and CD-ROM drivers installed in System folder.

500   Title from disc label.

500[b]   Production credits: Director, David Miller ; producers, Peter Bogdanoff, Wendy Bricht.

500   Digital recording of the music.

520[c]   Combines the interactivity of HyperCard with a compact audio disc to explore Mozart's music, including the biographical and historical circumstances of its creation, using text, graphics and audio examples.

500   "CDAC-012800"

020[c]   15559402172

• •

Access points: 700 10 Mozart, Wolfgang Amadeus, $d 1756-1791.
700 10 Winter, Robert, $d 1945-
700 11 Mozart, Wolfgang Amadeus, $d 1756-1791 $t Quartets, $m strings, $n K. 465, $r C major.
710 20 Angeles Quartet
710 20 Voyager Company
740 01 Dissonant   *(variant title)*

---

[a] All subject work and several 0xx fields have been omitted from this record.

[b] After MARC format integration this "Credits:" note would be tagged 508.

[c] The 020 and 520 are tagged with the understanding that display and print constants for national and local bibliographic systems have been taken into account.

GLOSSARY

This glossary contains definitions for special terms used in the Guidelines for Bibliographic Description of Interactive Multimedia. *Most cataloging related terms used in these guidelines are also terms used in AACR2R and defined in AACR2R's glossary; those definitions are not duplicated here. As appropriate, a reference is made from definitions for terms in this glossary to related terms defined in the AACR2R glossary. If additional assistance in understanding interactive multimedia concepts is needed, Appendix E provides a listing of published technical dictionaries, texts with glossaries, and other resources.*

Barcode. *See* Laser barcode.

CAV. Constant Angular Velocity. In optical disc storage systems, the format used for discs which require a drive that keeps disc rotation speed constant and synchronized with television vertical frequency. In comparison to CLV, CAV allows perfect still frames and improves random access capabilities (including supporting frame-by-frame access) and interactivity, but reduces storage capacity. *See also* CLV.

CD. Compact Disc. *See* Compact audio disc.

CD-A. Compact Disc-Audio. *See* Compact audio disc.

CD-DA. Compact Disc-Digital Audio. *See* Compact audio disc.

CD-I. Compact Disc-Interactive™. *See* Computer optical disc.

CD-R. Compact Disc Recordable.   *See* Computer optical disc.

CD-ROM. Compact Disc Read-Only Memory.   *See* Computer optical disc.

CD-ROM-XA. Compact Disc Read-Only Memory Extended Architecture.   *See* Computer optical disc.

CLV. Constant linear velocity.   In optical disc storage systems, the format used for compact audio discs, CD-ROM, some videodiscs, and other media, in which a disc rotates at varying speeds to ensure a constant data transfer rate. CLV does not permit random access to each frame unless a player with digital memory or other computing device can simulate clear scanning and freeze-frames. CLV reduces interactivity. On videodiscs, CLV increases storage capacity and so permits extended play. *See also* CAV.

Compact audio disc.   An optical, digital audio compact disc. Also known as *compact disc-audio* (CD-A), or *compact disc-digital audio* (CD-DA), or *compact disc* (CD).

Compact disc.   A general term used to describe any laser-encoded optical disc with a diameter of 5 inches or less. The term is used most often to refer to either compact audio discs or computer optical discs.

Computer disc.   *See* Computer optical disc.

Computer disk.   A magnetic disk used for storing computer data and programs. Information is stored on the disk surface in the form of magnetized spots. Computer disks come in various sizes. Also known as *floppy disk, computer diskette* or *floppy diskette.* (Spelling of disk with "k" is for describing magnetically encoded computer disks.)

Computer optical disc.   An optical disc used for storing information. Information is stored as a series of laser-burned micron-sized holes (pits) on a special recording layer. Recorded data is read optically. A computer optical disc may include computer files only, or computer files and other data (e.g., digital audio encoded for playback on a compact audio disc player). Commonly encountered computer optical disc formats are CD-A, CD-I, CD-R, CD-ROM, CD-ROM-XA, Photo CD. (Spelling of disc with "c" is for describing optically encoded computer discs.)

Computer magneto-optical disc (MOD).   A specialized optical disc storing information via a combination optical/magnetic data-writing system. A series of micron-sized spots on a special thermo-magnetically sensitive recording layer is used to store the data. Recorded data is read optically. MODs, unlike most other optical computer discs, are re-writable (i.e., data may be added, erased, and old data may be written over). MODs have greater storage capacity than computer magnetic disks. Most commonly known as *magneto-optical disc* (MOD). Commonly encountered computer magneto-optical disc formats are MO, O-ROM. (Spelling of disc with "c" is for describing magneto-optical computer discs.)

Disc.   *See* Compact disc, Compact audio disc, Computer optical disc, Computer magneto-optical disc.

Disk.   *See* Computer disk.

Floppy disk/diskette.   *See* Computer disk.

Graphical User Interface (GUI).   A graphic-based (i.e., windows, icons, etc.) software interface for video, computer or interactive multimedia systems. Users generally use a mouse or other pointing device to issue commands to and otherwise interact with the system or application.

Hyperlink.   A software link or association created using HyperCard™ or similar programs. Hyperlinks make connections so that the user may follow or create various pathways through related text, sound, images, etc.

Hypermedia.   *See* Interactive multimedia.

Interactive multimedia.   Media residing in one or more physical carriers (videodiscs, computer disks, computer optical discs, compact discs, etc.) or on computer networks. Interactive multimedia must exhibit both of these characteristics: (1) user controlled, nonlinear navigation using computer technology; and (2) the combination of two or more media (audio, text, graphics, images, animation, and video) that the user manipulates to control the order and/or nature of the presentation. *See also* Interactive multimedia work, Nonlinear navigation. *Compare* with Multimedia entry in AACR2R glossary.

Interactive multimedia work.   The whole intellectual content of an interactive multimedia entity, which forms the basis for a single bibliographic description. The interactive multimedia work may comprise one or more kinds of entities or a collection or compilation of various entities that may or may not have been published or issued at the same time or by the same issuing body. *See also* Interactive multimedia. *Compare* with Multimedia entry in AACR2R glossary.

Laser barcode.   A standard for encoding information in printed barcodes that can be used with barcode readable players to retrieve images or episodes from videodiscs. Laser Barcode 1 (LB) used a limited number of player and videodisc control features, while Laser Barcode 2 (LB2) uses an expanded set.

Levels I and II videodiscs.   Level I videodisc (usually in CLV format) and Level II videodiscs (usually in CAV format) are videodiscs carrying analog signals with limited user control functions which do not qualify as interactive multimedia, although they can be a component in interactive multimedia works when control functions are relocated to an external computer with companion software.

Level III videodisc.   A 12-inch optical disc carrying analog signals and running on a videodisc player that relocates control functions to an external computer with companion software, allowing users to change the content and dynamics of the presentation interactively. Level III videodiscs are usually in CAV format. Information can appear on a video or computer screen, or on a combined screen (through graphic overlay programming). Videodisc players accommodate many types of peripherals (e.g., light pens, touch screens, special printers, modems, etc.). Some Level II videodiscs can be upgraded to interactive Level III. Information about levels is frequently stated or implicit in the chief source of information.

Levels IV and V videodiscs. Levels IV and V videodiscs are enhanced Level III interactive videodiscs; locus of control remains with an external computer and companion software. Not widely available.

Media. A collective term for audio, text, graphics, images, animation, video, etc., that reside in one or more physical carriers or on an information network.

MIDI.   Musical Instrumental Digital Interface. *See* Sound board.

MO.   Magneto-optical. *See* Computer magneto-optical disc.

MOD.   Magneto-optical disc. *See* Computer magneto-optical disc.

MPC™. A licensed trademark of the Multimedia PC Marketing Council. Designed to assure hardware and software compliance with a commonly accepted minimum standard hardware/software platform (including sound boards, CD-ROM drives and Windows) for IBM and compatible computers. MPC and MPC-2 trademarked products are also subject to change when revised standards are issued for multimedia hardware/software products built for the IBM PC, IBM PC-compatible, DOS, and Windows products.

Nonlinear navigation. The ability of the user to determine freely the order of information retrieval in an interactive multimedia work. In an interactive multimedia work, the user may easily move through and explore the content of the work by choosing to move among points of information and existing pathways or links, altering those existing linkages and/or creating new linkages in the process. Hyperlinks or similar mechanisms make nonlinear navigation possible. (Users also have the option of following prescribed or preset pathways and links, if desired.)

Optical disc. *See* Computer optical disc.

O-ROM.   Optical Read-Only Memory. *See* Computer magneto-optical disc.

Photo CD. A computer optical disc that has digitized photographs. Photo CDs come in several formats. A master format contains images that can be displayed from a Photo CD player, CD-I player, or on a computer from a CD-ROM if the computer also has companion software. A portfolio format presents pictures with accompanying audio and is intended for more limited use.

QuickTime™. A software extension program developed by Apple Computer for integrating sound, animation and video into computer applications. QuickTime compresses and decompresses video and synchronizes audio with the video sequences. There is a QuickTime version for IBM and compatible computers running Windows, which is called QuickTime for Windows; Microsoft has its own software, called Video for Windows, that provides similar compression on IBM and compatibles.

Sound board. A computer hardware device (usually an add-on circuit board) that gives a computer the capability of playing and recording voice, music, and other sounds. Sound boards may also be capable of synthesizing music, voice, etc., mixing synthesized and played-back sound. If equipped with a Musical Instrument Digital Interface (MIDI) I/O (input-output) port, sound boards allow the user to control certain *musical instruments* connected to the computer. Sometimes referred to as *audio board* or spelled *soundboard*. Commonly encountered sound board brands/formats include Sound Blaster, Sound Blaster Pro, AdLib, Pro AudioSpectrum. Less frequently referred to as sound cards.

Ultimedia™. A trademark name for IBM's interactive multimedia products, which indicates a multimedia standard for IBM hardware and software similar to that of the MPC standard.

Video for Windows. A software extension program for compression developed by Microsoft for IBM and compatible computers running Windows. Video for Windows digitally records and plays back video and accompanying audio. Apple Computer has similar software called QuickTime for Macintosh computers.

Videodisc. Any videorecording carrying analog information on disc. Most current videodiscs are laser optical. In the past, other systems (e.g., capacitance electrical) have also been used. *See also* CAV, CLV, Level I and II videodiscs, Level III videodisc, Level IV and V videodiscs. *Compare* with Videorecording in AACR2R glossary.

Work (Interactive multimedia). *See* Interactive multimedia work.

SELECTED, ANNOTATED BIBLIOGRAPHY
DICTIONARIES, TEXTS WITH GLOSSARIES, AND OTHER RESOURCE MATERIALS ON INTERACTIVE MULTIMEDIA

Dictionaries

Freedman, Alan. *The Computer Glossary: The Complete Illustrated Desk Reference.* **6th ed. New York: AMACOM, 1993. 174p.**

A glossary plus computer literacy guide. Concise, readable, providing meaningful definitions, including terms associated with interactive multimedia. The book helps "to make sense out of the [computer] industry in general."

Microsoft Press Computer **Dictionary. 2nd ed. Redmond, WA: Microsoft Press, 1994. 392 p.**

Well-written definitions including helpful explanatory paragraphs, illustrations and a pronunciation guide. Discusses terms related to interactive multimedia as well as other computer terms. "For people who work with microcomputers but are not computer professionals."

Multimedia and Related Technologies: A Glossary of Terms. **Rev. ed. Falls Church, VA: Monitor Information Services, 1991. 67 p.**

Pamphlet-sized, with precisely worded definitions for terms relating to interactive video, multimedia computers, etc. Defines acronyms and abbreviations separately at end.

Pfaffenberger, Bryan. *Que's Computer User's Dictionary.* **3rd ed. Carmel, IN: Que, 1992. 656 p.**

A practical, almost pocket-sized guide, with clearly written paragraphs mixing non-technical and technical language for novice and advanced consumers alike. Includes interactive multimedia concepts, hints and cautionary advice.

Spencer, Donald. *Webster's New World Dictionary of Computer Terms.* **4th ed. New York: Prentice Hall, 1992. 458 p.**

A ready reference, pocket-sized collection of 5,000 very briefly defined terms for the beginning computer user, including interactive multimedia concepts. Be aware: some definitions are so brief as to be almost misleading. May need to be consulted in conjunction with another, more detailed dictionary.

Williams, Laurie and Robert Schleiffer, eds.; Craig LaGrow, publisher. *The Multimedia Dictionary.* **Petaluma, CA: Global Intermedia, 1992. 243 p.**

Clearly explains meanings for terms associated with multimedia for a variety of disciplines; each term is graphically associated with its industry by icons.

Williams, Robin with Steve Cummings. *Jargon: An Informal Dictionary of Computer Terms.* **Berkeley, CA: Peachpit Press, 1993. 676 p.**

Lengthy paragraphs define most terms. Excellent index. "For the beginning to average computer user, with the information necessary to get your everyday work accomplished." Includes interactive multimedia concepts; not a resource for precise technical explanations.

Texts with Glossaries, and Other Resource Materials on Interactive Multimedia

Addie, Chris, ed. *A Survey of Distributed Multimedia Research, Standards and Products.* **Edinburgh: Edinburgh University Computing Service, 1993. RARE Project OBR (92) 46v2**

A worldwide 1992 survey of cross-platform distributed interactive multimedia computer networking projects. The introduction defines terms and concepts; text contains research, standards, and lists of distributed multimedia works. Intended to be kept up-to-date.

Berger, Jeff. *The Desktop Multimedia Bible.* **New York: ABC News InterActive, 1993. 635 p.**

Geared to creators of multimedia; thoroughly discusses the processes and technologies used in creating interactive multimedia. Lacks formal glossary but includes many clear definitions throughout text. Excellent bibliography for additional reading. Not for novices.

Haynes, George R. *Opening Minds: the Evolution of Videodiscs & Interactive Learning.* **Dubuque, IA: Kendall/Hunt, 1989. 159 p.**

Historical, but still useful, offering a nine-page glossary for videodiscs including definitions for interactive video levels and related video terms. Text (160 pages) examines video and optical technologies and standards. Includes bibliography.

Hoffstetter, Fred Thomas. *Computer Literacy for Musicians.* **Englewood Cliffs, NJ: Prentice Hall, 1989. 351 p.**

Includes a six-page glossary along with chapters on music and computers; interactive videodiscs; music composition; and analysis programming; in a 300-page text.

Lambert, Steve, and Jane Sallis, eds. *CD-I and Interactive Video Technology.* **Indianapolis, IN: H.W. Sams, 1987. 206 p.**

Dated, yet offers a still-valid nine-page glossary for CD-I and related terms. Two-hundred-page text explores design parameters, standards, the future; historical information remains useful.

Locatis, Craig. *An Interactive Multimedia Technology Primer.* **Bethesda, MD: U.S. Dept. of Health & Human Services, Public Health Service, National Institutes of Health, 1993. 23 p.**

One of the leading experts in the field thoroughly explains interactive multimedia technologies, providing useful definitions for associated terms in this report.

Oblinger, Diana. *Introduction to Multimedia in Instruction.* **Chapel Hill: The Institute for Academic Technology, 1992. TPR-03. 12 p.**

This separately published technical report clearly introduces the topic of interactive multimedia, including definitions and the importance of educational applications.

Tway, Linda E. *Welcome to Multimedia.* **New York: Management Information Source Press, 1992. 322 p.**

A twenty-two page highly readable glossary backs up an easy-to-understand text geared to the novice. Text includes overview, uses, hardware/software, construction and applications. Excellent graphics.